Girl boss

Your Bag!

A Financial Goals Planner & Expense Tracker

Created by Jennipher L. Kincade

MJU Publishing, LLC

Girl, Boss Your Bag! A Financial Goals Planner & Expense Tracker

ISBN: 979-8-9871267-6-9

Hey Ladies,

It's time for us to boss our bags! That is exactly why this planner was created. With the "Girl, Boss Your Bag!" 18-month planner, you will be able to keep track of your monthly expenses, check off which bills you have paid and see what still needs to be paid, get a visual of your income, and have a space to set your goals while simultaneously seeing the progress you've made reaching your financial goals. Using this planner consistently will help keep you on track so that you don't miss paying bills on time or overestimate your income to output ratio. It's important to keep track of your finances, but it is also important to stay encouraged and motivated while you are on your financial journey. That is why for each month, there is a page of colorful "sticky notes" where you can write down reminders, goals, and inspirational words for yourself. There are also pages included for every month that allows you to check off monthly goals that have absolutely nothing to do with finances because real life goes beyond just "the bag." Each month is left blank so that you can start during any month of the year. No more waiting until January of the next year. When it comes to taking control and making changes to better your life, start wherever you find yourself. Let's be clear, this planner is not magic. It is a fun, uniquely designed tool that will work for you when you do the necessary work. Get ready to stay on track, make goals, track your progression, be inspired, and boss your bag!

Jennipher Lynette

I truly believe that butterflies are a representation of new beginnings. I hope to see you fly!

My Monthly Expenses

MONTH: March 2024

MY MONTHLY INCOME:

PAY DATE	INCOME SOURCE	AMOUNT	☑
03/01/24	Primary Employment	$1500	☑
03/12/24	Part-time job	$700	☑
03/16/24	Primary Employment	$1500	☑
03/31/24	Primary Employment	$1500	☐

RECURRING MONTHLY EXPENSES

DUE DATE	EXPENSE	AMOUNT	☑
03/01/24	Mortgage	$1175	☑
03/01/24	Car Insurance	$110	☑
03/09/24	Electric Bill	$88.27	☑
03/12/24	Cable/Internet/Phone Service	$158.21	☑
03/15/24	Car Note	$375.80	☑
03/15/24	Monthly Groceries	$260.00	☑
03/31/24	Water/Trash/Sewer	$93.45	☐
			☐

MISCELLANEOUS EXPENSES

DUE DATE	EXPENSE	AMOUNT	☑
03/15/24	Hair Appointment	$115.00	☑
03/25/24	Car Service/Oil Change	$84.00	☐
			☐
			☐

TOTAL MONTHLY EXPENSES: $2459.73   TOTAL MONTHLY INCOME: $5200

MONEY
GOALS & ACCOMPLISHMENTS

THIS MONTH'S FINANCIAL GOAL(S) ☑

- Deposit $300 to savings account ☑
- Learn more about investment opportunities ☐
- Do not go out to eat more than 2 times this month ☐

SOMETHING THAT IMPROVED THIS MONTH:

I reduced the number of misc. expenses for the month

A POSITIVE REMINDER FOR MYSELF:

No one gets everything right every time. Allow myself grace to make mistakes and learn from them.

WHAT DID I LEARN THIS MONTH ABOUT MYSELF AND/OR MONEY?

I am capable of financial discipline.

HOW CAN I BE BETTER NEXT MONTH?

Find the right balance of discipline and enjoyment. Learn how I can enjoy the fruits of my labor without placing myself in a position to be in financial discomfort later.

Taking Time to Nurture Me

 I set reasonable goals for myself this month

I set and enforced boundaries to protect my peace and my energy

 I took the time this month to do something that was just for me

 I participated in an enjoyable hobby or special interest that I hadn't done in a while

I took a few minutes each day to quiet my mind and have meditation or prayer time

 I made at least one healthy meal choice per day this month

 I took the initiative to only engage in social interactions that were positive

I spoke kindly to or of myself each day this month

I exercised at least 3 times per week this month

I went for a 30 minute walk one day per week

I tried something new this month.

I found a new routine that saves me an hour of time each day.

I spent more quality time with my partner this month.

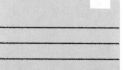

Just Thinking on Paper...

Use this page as your personal notepad to jot
down any thoughts or ideas you may have
from calculations, estimations, or what was on
your mind as a travel goal
that month. It can even be a grocery list. Use
this notepad for whatever you like!

Are you ready to start? Let's go!

My Monthly Expenses

MONTH: _____

MY MONTHLY INCOME:

PAY DATE	INCOME SOURCE	AMOUNT	☑
			☐
			☐
			☐
			☐

RECURRING MONTHLY EXPENSES

DUE DATE	EXPENSE	AMOUNT	☑
			☐
			☐
			☐
			☐
			☐
			☐
			☐
			☐

MISCELLANEOUS EXPENSES

DUE DATE	EXPENSE	AMOUNT	☑
			☐
			☐
			☐
			☐

TOTAL MONTHLY EXPENSES: TOTAL MONTHLY INCOME:

MONEY
GOALS&ACCOMPLISHMENTS

THIS MONTH'S FINANCIAL GOAL(S) ☑

- ☐
- ☐
- ☐

SOMETHING THAT IMPROVED THIS MONTH:

A POSITIVE REMINDER FOR MYSELF:

WHAT DID I LEARN THIS MONTH ABOUT MYSELF AND/OR MONEY?

HOW CAN I BE BETTER NEXT MONTH?

Taking Time to Nurture Me

I set reasonable goals for myself this month

I set and enforced boundaries to protect my peace and my energy

I took the time this month to do something that was just for me

I participated in an enjoyable hobby or special interest that I hadn't done in a while

I took a few minutes each day to quiet my mind and have meditation or prayer time

I made at least one healthy meal choice per day this month

I took the initiative to only engage in social interactions that were positive

I spoke kindly to or of myself each day this month

I exercised at least 3 times per week this month

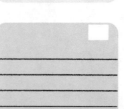

Just Thinking on Paper...

My Monthly Expenses

MONTH: _____

MY MONTHLY INCOME:

PAY DATE	INCOME SOURCE	AMOUNT	☑
			☐
			☐
			☐
			☐

RECURRING MONTHLY EXPENSES

DUE DATE	EXPENSE	AMOUNT	☑
			☐
			☐
			☐
			☐
			☐
			☐
			☐
			☐

MISCELLANEOUS EXPENSES

DUE DATE	EXPENSE	AMOUNT	☑
			☐
			☐
			☐
			☐

TOTAL MONTHLY EXPENSES: TOTAL MONTHLY INCOME:

MONEY
GOALS&ACCOMPLISHMENTS

THIS MONTH'S FINANCIAL GOAL(S)

☑

- ☐
- ☐
- ☐

SOMETHING THAT IMPROVED THIS MONTH:

A POSITIVE REMINDER FOR MYSELF:

WHAT DID I LEARN THIS MONTH ABOUT MYSELF AND/OR MONEY?

HOW CAN I BE BETTER NEXT MONTH?

Taking Time to Nurture Me

I set reasonable goals for myself this month

I set and enforced boundaries to protect my peace and my energy

I took the time this month to do something that was just for me

I participated in an enjoyable hobby or special interest that I hadn't done in a while

I took a few minutes each day to quiet my mind and have meditation or prayer time

I made at least one healthy meal choice per day this month

I took the initiative to only engage in social interactions that were positive

I spoke kindly to or of myself each day this month

I exercised at least 3 times per week this month

Just Thinking on Paper...

My Monthly Expenses

MONTH: _____

MY MONTHLY INCOME:

PAY DATE	INCOME SOURCE	AMOUNT	☑
			☐
			☐
			☐
			☐

RECURRING MONTHLY EXPENSES

DUE DATE	EXPENSE	AMOUNT	☑
			☐
			☐
			☐
			☐
			☐
			☐
			☐
			☐

MISCELLANEOUS EXPENSES

DUE DATE	EXPENSE	AMOUNT	☑
			☐
			☐
			☐
			☐

TOTAL MONTHLY EXPENSES: TOTAL MONTHLY INCOME:

MONEY
GOALS&ACCOMPLISHMENTS

THIS MONTH'S FINANCIAL GOAL(S)

☑

- ☐
- ☐
- ☐

SOMETHING THAT IMPROVED THIS MONTH:

A POSITIVE REMINDER FOR MYSELF:

WHAT DID I LEARN THIS MONTH ABOUT MYSELF AND/OR MONEY?

HOW CAN I BE BETTER NEXT MONTH?

Taking Time to Nurture Me

I set reasonable goals for myself this month

I set and enforced boundaries to protect my peace and my energy

I took the time this month to do something that was just for me

I participated in an enjoyable hobby or special interest that I hadn't done in a while

I took a few minutes each day to quiet my mind and have meditation or prayer time

I made at least one healthy meal choice per day this month

I took the initiative to only engage in social interactions that were positive

I spoke kindly to or of myself each day this month

I exercised at least 3 times per week this month

Just Thinking on Paper...

My Monthly Expenses

MONTH: _____

MY MONTHLY INCOME:

PAY DATE	INCOME SOURCE	AMOUNT	☑
			☐
			☐
			☐
			☐

RECURRING MONTHLY EXPENSES

DUE DATE	EXPENSE	AMOUNT	☑
			☐
			☐
			☐
			☐
			☐
			☐
			☐
			☐

MISCELLANEOUS EXPENSES

DUE DATE	EXPENSE	AMOUNT	☑
			☐
			☐
			☐
			☐

TOTAL MONTHLY EXPENSES: TOTAL MONTHLY INCOME:

MONEY
GOALS&ACCOMPLISHMENTS

THIS MONTH'S FINANCIAL GOAL(S)

☑

- ☐
- ☐
- ☐

SOMETHING THAT IMPROVED THIS MONTH:

A POSITIVE REMINDER FOR MYSELF:

WHAT DID I LEARN THIS MONTH ABOUT MYSELF AND/OR MONEY?

HOW CAN I BE BETTER NEXT MONTH?

Taking Time to Nurture Me

I set reasonable goals for myself this month

I set and enforced boundaries to protect my peace and my energy

I took the time this month to do something that was just for me

I participated in an enjoyable hobby or special interest that I hadn't done in a while

I took a few minutes each day to quiet my mind and have meditation or prayer time

I made at least one healthy meal choice per day this month

I took the initiative to only engage in social interactions that were positive

I spoke kindly to or of myself each day this month

I exercised at least 3 times per week this month

Just Thinking on Paper...

My Monthly Expenses

MONTH: _____

MY MONTHLY INCOME:

PAY DATE	INCOME SOURCE	AMOUNT	☑
			☐
			☐
			☐
			☐

RECURRING MONTHLY EXPENSES

DUE DATE	EXPENSE	AMOUNT	☑
			☐
			☐
			☐
			☐
			☐
			☐
			☐
			☐

MISCELLANEOUS EXPENSES

DUE DATE	EXPENSE	AMOUNT	☑
			☐
			☐
			☐
			☐

TOTAL MONTHLY EXPENSES: TOTAL MONTHLY INCOME:

MONEY
GOALS&ACCOMPLISHMENTS

THIS MONTH'S FINANCIAL GOAL(S)

☑

- ☐
- ☐
- ☐

SOMETHING THAT IMPROVED THIS MONTH:

A POSITIVE REMINDER FOR MYSELF:

WHAT DID I LEARN THIS MONTH ABOUT MYSELF AND/OR MONEY?

HOW CAN I BE BETTER NEXT MONTH?

Taking Time to Nurture Me

I set reasonable goals for myself this month

I set and enforced boundaries to protect my peace and my energy

I took the time this month to do something that was just for me

I participated in an enjoyable hobby or special interest that I hadn't done in a while

I took a few minutes each day to quiet my mind and have meditation or prayer time

I made at least one healthy meal choice per day this month

I took the initiative to only engage in social interactions that were positive

I spoke kindly to or of myself each day this month

I exercised at least 3 times per week this month

Just Thinking on Paper...

My Monthly Expenses

MONTH: _____

MY MONTHLY INCOME:

PAY DATE	INCOME SOURCE	AMOUNT	☑
			☐
			☐
			☐
			☐

RECURRING MONTHLY EXPENSES

DUE DATE	EXPENSE	AMOUNT	☑
			☐
			☐
			☐
			☐
			☐
			☐
			☐
			☐

MISCELLANEOUS EXPENSES

DUE DATE	EXPENSE	AMOUNT	☑
			☐
			☐
			☐
			☐

TOTAL MONTHLY EXPENSES: TOTAL MONTHLY INCOME:

MONEY
GOALS&ACCOMPLISHMENTS

THIS MONTH'S FINANCIAL GOAL(S)

☑

- ☐
- ☐
- ☐

SOMETHING THAT IMPROVED THIS MONTH:

A POSITIVE REMINDER FOR MYSELF:

WHAT DID I LEARN THIS MONTH ABOUT MYSELF AND/OR MONEY?

HOW CAN I BE BETTER NEXT MONTH?

Taking Time to Nurture Me

I set reasonable goals for myself this month

I set and enforced boundaries to protect my peace and my energy

I took the time this month to do something that was just for me

I participated in an enjoyable hobby or special interest that I hadn't done in a while

I took a few minutes each day to quiet my mind and have meditation or prayer time

I made at least one healthy meal choice per day this month

I took the initiative to only engage in social interactions that were positive

I spoke kindly to or of myself each day this month

I exercised at least 3 times per week this month

Just Thinking on Paper...

My Monthly Expenses

MONTH: _____

MY MONTHLY INCOME:

PAY DATE	INCOME SOURCE	AMOUNT	☑
			☐
			☐
			☐
			☐

RECURRING MONTHLY EXPENSES

DUE DATE	EXPENSE	AMOUNT	☑
			☐
			☐
			☐
			☐
			☐
			☐
			☐
			☐

MISCELLANEOUS EXPENSES

DUE DATE	EXPENSE	AMOUNT	☑
			☐
			☐
			☐
			☐

TOTAL MONTHLY EXPENSES: TOTAL MONTHLY INCOME:

MONEY
GOALS&ACCOMPLISHMENTS

THIS MONTH'S FINANCIAL GOAL(S)

☑

- ☐
- ☐
- ☐

SOMETHING THAT IMPROVED THIS MONTH:

A POSITIVE REMINDER FOR MYSELF:

WHAT DID I LEARN THIS MONTH ABOUT MYSELF AND/OR MONEY?

HOW CAN I BE BETTER NEXT MONTH?

Taking Time to Nurture Me

I set reasonable goals for myself this month

I set and enforced boundaries to protect my peace and my energy

I took the time this month to do something that was just for me

I participated in an enjoyable hobby or special interest that I hadn't done in a while

I took a few minutes each day to quiet my mind and have meditation or prayer time

I made at least one healthy meal choice per day this month

I took the initiative to only engage in social interactions that were positive

I spoke kindly to or of myself each day this month

I exercised at least 3 times per week this month

Just Thinking on Paper...

My Monthly Expenses

MONTH: _____

MY MONTHLY INCOME:

PAY DATE	INCOME SOURCE	AMOUNT	☑
			☐
			☐
			☐
			☐

RECURRING MONTHLY EXPENSES

DUE DATE	EXPENSE	AMOUNT	☑
			☐
			☐
			☐
			☐
			☐
			☐
			☐
			☐

MISCELLANEOUS EXPENSES

DUE DATE	EXPENSE	AMOUNT	☑
			☐
			☐
			☐
			☐

TOTAL MONTHLY EXPENSES: TOTAL MONTHLY INCOME:

MONEY
GOALS&ACCOMPLISHMENTS

THIS MONTH'S FINANCIAL GOAL(S)

☑

- ☐
- ☐
- ☐

SOMETHING THAT IMPROVED THIS MONTH:

A POSITIVE REMINDER FOR MYSELF:

WHAT DID I LEARN THIS MONTH ABOUT MYSELF AND/OR MONEY?

HOW CAN I BE BETTER NEXT MONTH?

Taking Time to Nurture Me

I set reasonable goals for myself this month

I set and enforced boundaries to protect my peace and my energy

I took the time this month to do something that was just for me

I participated in an enjoyable hobby or special interest that I hadn't done in a while

I took a few minutes each day to quiet my mind and have meditation or prayer time

I made at least one healthy meal choice per day this month

I took the initiative to only engage in social interactions that were positive

I spoke kindly to or of myself each day this month

I exercised at least 3 times per week this month

Just Thinking on Paper...

My Monthly Expenses

MONTH: _____

MY MONTHLY INCOME:

PAY DATE	INCOME SOURCE	AMOUNT	☑
			☐
			☐
			☐
			☐

RECURRING MONTHLY EXPENSES

DUE DATE	EXPENSE	AMOUNT	☑
			☐
			☐
			☐
			☐
			☐
			☐
			☐
			☐

MISCELLANEOUS EXPENSES

DUE DATE	EXPENSE	AMOUNT	☑
			☐
			☐
			☐
			☐

TOTAL MONTHLY EXPENSES: TOTAL MONTHLY INCOME:

MONEY
GOALS & ACCOMPLISHMENTS

THIS MONTH'S FINANCIAL GOAL(S)

☑

☐

☐

☐

SOMETHING THAT IMPROVED THIS MONTH:

A POSITIVE REMINDER FOR MYSELF:

WHAT DID I LEARN THIS MONTH ABOUT MYSELF AND/OR MONEY?

HOW CAN I BE BETTER NEXT MONTH?

Taking Time to Nurture Me

I set reasonable goals for myself this month

I set and enforced boundaries to protect my peace and my energy

I took the time this month to do something that was just for me

I participated in an enjoyable hobby or special interest that I hadn't done in a while

I took a few minutes each day to quiet my mind and have meditation or prayer time

I made at least one healthy meal choice per day this month

I took the initiative to only engage in social interactions that were positive

I spoke kindly to or of myself each day this month

I exercised at least 3 times per week this month

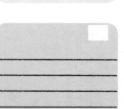

Just Thinking on Paper...

My Monthly Expenses

MONTH: _____

MY MONTHLY INCOME:

PAY DATE	INCOME SOURCE	AMOUNT	☑
			☐
			☐
			☐
			☐

RECURRING MONTHLY EXPENSES

DUE DATE	EXPENSE	AMOUNT	☑
			☐
			☐
			☐
			☐
			☐
			☐
			☐
			☐

MISCELLANEOUS EXPENSES

DUE DATE	EXPENSE	AMOUNT	☑
			☐
			☐
			☐
			☐

TOTAL MONTHLY EXPENSES: TOTAL MONTHLY INCOME:

MONEY
GOALS&ACCOMPLISHMENTS

THIS MONTH'S FINANCIAL GOAL(S)

☑

- ☐
- ☐
- ☐

SOMETHING THAT IMPROVED THIS MONTH:

A POSITIVE REMINDER FOR MYSELF:

WHAT DID I LEARN THIS MONTH ABOUT MYSELF AND/OR MONEY?

HOW CAN I BE BETTER NEXT MONTH?

Taking Time to Nurture Me

I set reasonable goals for myself this month

I set and enforced boundaries to protect my peace and my energy

I took the time this month to do something that was just for me

I participated in an enjoyable hobby or special interest that I hadn't done in a while

I took a few minutes each day to quiet my mind and have meditation or prayer time

I made at least one healthy meal choice per day this month

I took the initiative to only engage in social interactions that were positive

I spoke kindly to or of myself each day this month

I exercised at least 3 times per week this month

Just Thinking on Paper...

My Monthly Expenses

MONTH: _____

MY MONTHLY INCOME:

PAY DATE	INCOME SOURCE	AMOUNT	☑
			☐
			☐
			☐
			☐

RECURRING MONTHLY EXPENSES

DUE DATE	EXPENSE	AMOUNT	☑
			☐
			☐
			☐
			☐
			☐
			☐
			☐
			☐

MISCELLANEOUS EXPENSES

DUE DATE	EXPENSE	AMOUNT	☑
			☐
			☐
			☐
			☐

TOTAL MONTHLY EXPENSES: TOTAL MONTHLY INCOME:

MONEY
GOALS&ACCOMPLISHMENTS

THIS MONTH'S FINANCIAL GOAL(S)

☑

- ☐
- ☐
- ☐

SOMETHING THAT IMPROVED THIS MONTH:

A POSITIVE REMINDER FOR MYSELF:

WHAT DID I LEARN THIS MONTH ABOUT MYSELF AND/OR MONEY?

HOW CAN I BE BETTER NEXT MONTH?

Taking Time to Nurture Me

I set reasonable goals for myself this month

I set and enforced boundaries to protect my peace and my energy

I took the time this month to do something that was just for me

I participated in an enjoyable hobby or special interest that I hadn't done in a while

I took a few minutes each day to quiet my mind and have meditation or prayer time

I made at least one healthy meal choice per day this month

I took the initiative to only engage in social interactions that were positive

I spoke kindly to or of myself each day this month

I exercised at least 3 times per week this month

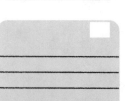

Just Thinking on Paper...

My Monthly Expenses

MONTH: _____

MY MONTHLY INCOME:

PAY DATE	INCOME SOURCE	AMOUNT	☑
			☐
			☐
			☐
			☐

RECURRING MONTHLY EXPENSES

DUE DATE	EXPENSE	AMOUNT	☑
			☐
			☐
			☐
			☐
			☐
			☐
			☐
			☐

MISCELLANEOUS EXPENSES

DUE DATE	EXPENSE	AMOUNT	☑
			☐
			☐
			☐
			☐

TOTAL MONTHLY EXPENSES: TOTAL MONTHLY INCOME:

MONEY
GOALS&ACCOMPLISHMENTS

THIS MONTH'S FINANCIAL GOAL(S)

☑

- ☐
- ☐
- ☐

SOMETHING THAT IMPROVED THIS MONTH:

A POSITIVE REMINDER FOR MYSELF:

WHAT DID I LEARN THIS MONTH ABOUT MYSELF AND/OR MONEY?

HOW CAN I BE BETTER NEXT MONTH?

Taking Time to Nurture Me

I set reasonable goals for myself this month

I set and enforced boundaries to protect my peace and my energy

I took the time this month to do something that was just for me

I participated in an enjoyable hobby or special interest that I hadn't done in a while

I took a few minutes each day to quiet my mind and have meditation or prayer time

I made at least one healthy meal choice per day this month

I took the initiative to only engage in social interactions that were positive

I spoke kindly to or of myself each day this month

I exercised at least 3 times per week this month

Just Thinking on Paper...

My Monthly Expenses

MONTH: _____

MY MONTHLY INCOME:

PAY DATE	INCOME SOURCE	AMOUNT	☑
			☐
			☐
			☐
			☐

RECURRING MONTHLY EXPENSES

DUE DATE	EXPENSE	AMOUNT	☑
			☐
			☐
			☐
			☐
			☐
			☐
			☐
			☐

MISCELLANEOUS EXPENSES

DUE DATE	EXPENSE	AMOUNT	☑
			☐
			☐
			☐
			☐

TOTAL MONTHLY EXPENSES: TOTAL MONTHLY INCOME:

MONEY
GOALS&ACCOMPLISHMENTS

THIS MONTH'S FINANCIAL GOAL(S) ☑

- ☐
- ☐
- ☐

SOMETHING THAT IMPROVED THIS
MONTH:

A POSITIVE REMINDER FOR
MYSELF:

WHAT DID I LEARN THIS MONTH
ABOUT MYSELF AND/OR MONEY?

HOW CAN I BE BETTER NEXT
MONTH?

Taking Time to Nurture Me

I set reasonable goals for myself this month

I set and enforced boundaries to protect my peace and my energy

I took the time this month to do something that was just for me

I participated in an enjoyable hobby or special interest that I hadn't done in a while

I took a few minutes each day to quiet my mind and have meditation or prayer time

I made at least one healthy meal choice per day this month

I took the initiative to only engage in social interactions that were positive

I spoke kindly to or of myself each day this month

I exercised at least 3 times per week this month

Just Thinking on Paper...

My Monthly Expenses

MONTH: _____

MY MONTHLY INCOME:

PAY DATE	INCOME SOURCE	AMOUNT	☑
			☐
			☐
			☐
			☐

RECURRING MONTHLY EXPENSES

DUE DATE	EXPENSE	AMOUNT	☑
			☐
			☐
			☐
			☐
			☐
			☐
			☐
			☐

MISCELLANEOUS EXPENSES

DUE DATE	EXPENSE	AMOUNT	☑
			☐
			☐
			☐
			☐

TOTAL MONTHLY EXPENSES: TOTAL MONTHLY INCOME:

MONEY
GOALS&ACCOMPLISHMENTS

THIS MONTH'S FINANCIAL GOAL(S) ☑

- ☐
- ☐
- ☐

SOMETHING THAT IMPROVED THIS MONTH:

A POSITIVE REMINDER FOR MYSELF:

WHAT DID I LEARN THIS MONTH ABOUT MYSELF AND/OR MONEY?

HOW CAN I BE BETTER NEXT MONTH?

Taking Time to Nurture Me

I set reasonable goals for myself this month

I set and enforced boundaries to protect my peace and my energy

I took the time this month to do something that was just for me

I participated in an enjoyable hobby or special interest that I hadn't done in a while

I took a few minutes each day to quiet my mind and have meditation or prayer time

I made at least one healthy meal choice per day this month

I took the initiative to only engage in social interactions that were positive

I spoke kindly to or of myself each day this month

I exercised at least 3 times per week this month

Just Thinking on Paper...

My Monthly Expenses

MONTH: _____

MY MONTHLY INCOME:

PAY DATE	INCOME SOURCE	AMOUNT	☑
			☐
			☐
			☐
			☐

RECURRING MONTHLY EXPENSES

DUE DATE	EXPENSE	AMOUNT	☑
			☐
			☐
			☐
			☐
			☐
			☐
			☐
			☐

MISCELLANEOUS EXPENSES

DUE DATE	EXPENSE	AMOUNT	☑
			☐
			☐
			☐
			☐

TOTAL MONTHLY EXPENSES: TOTAL MONTHLY INCOME:

MONEY
GOALS&ACCOMPLISHMENTS

THIS MONTH'S FINANCIAL GOAL(S) ☑

- ☐
- ☐
- ☐

SOMETHING THAT IMPROVED THIS MONTH:

A POSITIVE REMINDER FOR MYSELF:

WHAT DID I LEARN THIS MONTH ABOUT MYSELF AND/OR MONEY?

HOW CAN I BE BETTER NEXT MONTH?

Taking Time to Nurture Me

I set reasonable goals for myself this month

I set and enforced boundaries to protect my peace and my energy

I took the time this month to do something that was just for me

I participated in an enjoyable hobby or special interest that I hadn't done in a while

I took a few minutes each day to quiet my mind and have meditation or prayer time

I made at least one healthy meal choice per day this month

I took the initiative to only engage in social interactions that were positive

I spoke kindly to or of myself each day this month

I exercised at least 3 times per week this month

Just Thinking on Paper...

My Monthly Expenses

MONTH: _____

MY MONTHLY INCOME:

PAY DATE	INCOME SOURCE	AMOUNT	☑
			☐
			☐
			☐
			☐

RECURRING MONTHLY EXPENSES

DUE DATE	EXPENSE	AMOUNT	☑
			☐
			☐
			☐
			☐
			☐
			☐
			☐
			☐

MISCELLANEOUS EXPENSES

DUE DATE	EXPENSE	AMOUNT	☑
			☐
			☐
			☐
			☐

TOTAL MONTHLY EXPENSES: TOTAL MONTHLY INCOME:

MONEY
GOALS&ACCOMPLISHMENTS

THIS MONTH'S FINANCIAL GOAL(S)

☑

- ☐
- ☐
- ☐

SOMETHING THAT IMPROVED THIS MONTH:

A POSITIVE REMINDER FOR MYSELF:

WHAT DID I LEARN THIS MONTH ABOUT MYSELF AND/OR MONEY?

HOW CAN I BE BETTER NEXT MONTH?

Taking Time to Nurture Me

I set reasonable goals for myself this month

I set and enforced boundaries to protect my peace and my energy

I took the time this month to do something that was just for me

I participated in an enjoyable hobby or special interest that I hadn't done in a while

I took a few minutes each day to quiet my mind and have meditation or prayer time

I made at least one healthy meal choice per day this month

I took the initiative to only engage in social interactions that were positive

I spoke kindly to or of myself each day this month

I exercised at least 3 times per week this month

Just Thinking on Paper...

My Monthly Expenses

MONTH: _____

MY MONTHLY INCOME:

PAY DATE	INCOME SOURCE	AMOUNT	☑
			☐
			☐
			☐
			☐

RECURRING MONTHLY EXPENSES

DUE DATE	EXPENSE	AMOUNT	☑
			☐
			☐
			☐
			☐
			☐
			☐
			☐
			☐

MISCELLANEOUS EXPENSES

DUE DATE	EXPENSE	AMOUNT	☑
			☐
			☐
			☐
			☐

TOTAL MONTHLY EXPENSES: TOTAL MONTHLY INCOME:

MONEY
GOALS&ACCOMPLISHMENTS

THIS MONTH'S FINANCIAL GOAL(S)

☑

- ☐
- ☐
- ☐

SOMETHING THAT IMPROVED THIS MONTH:

A POSITIVE REMINDER FOR MYSELF:

WHAT DID I LEARN THIS MONTH ABOUT MYSELF AND/OR MONEY?

HOW CAN I BE BETTER NEXT MONTH?

Taking Time to Nurture Me

I set reasonable goals for myself this month

I set and enforced boundaries to protect my peace and my energy

I took the time this month to do something that was just for me

I participated in an enjoyable hobby or special interest that I hadn't done in a while

I took a few minutes each day to quiet my mind and have meditation or prayer time

I made at least one healthy meal choice per day this month

I took the initiative to only engage in social interactions that were positive

I spoke kindly to or of myself each day this month

I exercised at least 3 times per week this month

Just Thinking on Paper...

My Monthly Expenses

MONTH: _____

MY MONTHLY INCOME:

PAY DATE	INCOME SOURCE	AMOUNT	☑
			☐
			☐
			☐
			☐

RECURRING MONTHLY EXPENSES

DUE DATE	EXPENSE	AMOUNT	☑
			☐
			☐
			☐
			☐
			☐
			☐
			☐
			☐

MISCELLANEOUS EXPENSES

DUE DATE	EXPENSE	AMOUNT	☑
			☐
			☐
			☐
			☐

TOTAL MONTHLY EXPENSES:　　　　TOTAL MONTHLY INCOME:

MONEY
GOALS&ACCOMPLISHMENTS

THIS MONTH'S FINANCIAL GOAL(S)

☑

- ☐
- ☐
- ☐

SOMETHING THAT IMPROVED THIS MONTH:

A POSITIVE REMINDER FOR MYSELF:

WHAT DID I LEARN THIS MONTH ABOUT MYSELF AND/OR MONEY?

HOW CAN I BE BETTER NEXT MONTH?

Taking Time to Nurture Me

I set reasonable goals for myself this month

I set and enforced boundaries to protect my peace and my energy

I took the time this month to do something that was just for me

I participated in an enjoyable hobby or special interest that I hadn't done in a while

I took a few minutes each day to quiet my mind and have meditation or prayer time

I made at least one healthy meal choice per day this month

I took the initiative to only engage in social interactions that were positive

I spoke kindly to or of myself each day this month

I exercised at least 3 times per week this month

Just Thinking on Paper...

Made in the USA
Columbia, SC
28 February 2024